Deepening

Pure awareness — that is awareness without content — has a slightly luminous quality. It's a quiet joy we can't hold or even adequately describe. All we can do is surrender into it.

Deepening:

Opening Awareness and Surrendering into Joy

Doug Kraft

Easing Awake Books

Published by Easing Awake Books, 2023
Carmichael, CA 95608
https://www.easingawake.com
January 14, 2024

ISBN: 978-1-7350737-4-3   paperback
ISBN: 978-1-7350737-5-0   e-book

Printed in the United States of America
5   4   3   2   1

also by Doug Kraft

Centering Home

Buddha's Map

Beginning the Journey

Kindness and Wisdom Practice

Meditator's Field Guide

Befriending the Mind

Resting in the Waves

Presence

Contents

Introduction

We shall not cease from exploration
And the end of all exploring
Will be to arrive where we started
And know the place for the first time.
— T. S. Eliot

Everything we experience comes through awareness. Another word for "awareness" is "consciousness." Everything we experience comes through consciousness. Deepening awareness and consciousness allow natural contentment and well-being to permeate our lives.

We humans have great a facility for language and concepts and the instinctual urges to use them, especially under stress. We may compose paragraphs or entire books to describe our experience, awareness, and consciousness. But at best, words are pointers, not the experience itself. Our ideas about experience are afterthoughts rather than forerunners.

A well-known parable tells of a man who lost his keys inside his house but looked for them under the streetlamp because the light was better outside.

If we want to deepen consciousness, we must first know where to look. The keys to awareness and consciousness cannot be found in the bright light of thinking. Consciousness arises out of primordial affective emotions. It grows out of what we feel. Neurologically it is rooted in the mid and lower brain rather than the higher neocortex.

To understand this, consider how all mammals appear to be conscious despite many species having no language beyond a few primitive calls. Hydrocephalic children have no neocortices and no language centers in their brains. Yet they have personalities, preferences, moods, and the ability to learn. Despite obvious cognitive deficits, they are aware and conscious.

While it seems easy to look for consciousness in the bright light of the intellect, ultimately our search will fail because the keys are within, far below the level of language and thought.

I've written extensively about meditative and contemplative practices that look beneath language and thought. Recently a mentee asked where, among those books, I describe exactly what to do in the moment. I was chagrined to realize that while I have given lots of hints, I have never described the instinctual framework I personally use to work directly with my own awareness and that of my students and clients. I hope this booklet begins to provide that context.

To reverse an old analogy, these pages engage the question "Once I have a map of the forest, how do I deal with this tree?"

One way to work with awareness is to look beyond cognition to the actual body-based feeling tones. To get a sense of this process, try this:

- Close your eyes to lessen external distractions and let the thinking mind settle.
- Now look to see what moods and emotions are pushing and pulling inside. Sometimes they are murky. Language may rush in with terms like "fear," "peacefulness," "anger," or "pensiveness." The verbiage doesn't have to be a problem if you know it points toward something deeper. You can gently shift attention to the raw body-feelings within by asking, "Is there a better word to point to this experience?"

• If the first word was "fear," a better pointer might be "worry," "anxiousness," or "shyness." If it was "peacefulness," a better handle might be "contentment" or "quiet." If it was "anger," a better term might be "irritation," "upset," or "fury."

• Using that approach, find a word that better matches your actual mood or feeling tone. Let it settle. Then set the second term aside and come back into the body-based experience again. Is there an even better pointer?

• Repeat the process until you find the language that best describes your inner sense. Use it to help open your awareness and relax into what arises.

Focusing

The American philosopher and psychologist Eugene Gendlin calls this "Focusing." It's a way of reaching beyond language to the nonverbal territory within. What I just described is a simplified version of Focusing. So before going further, it would be helpful to look at how the practice of Deepening evolved out of Gendlin's work.

Eugene Gendlin bridged some of the gaps between philosophy and psychology and between serious academic study and popular self-help. He was a student and colleague of Carl Rogers, who is famous for his "client-centered therapy," which was in turn deeply influenced by the collaboration between Rogers and Gendlin.

In the 1950s and '60s, Gendlin researched a wide range of schools of psychotherapy to ascertain which of them produced the most positive and lasting outcomes for patients.

At that time there were three major branches of psychotherapy in the United States. The oldest was psychoanalysis as exemplified by Freud, Jung, and the neo-Freudians. The second oldest branch was Behaviorism, as found in John Watson's classical conditioning, B. F. Skinner's operant conditioning, William Glasser's reality therapy, and others. The newest branch was the then-emerging "third wave" of humanistic psychology, which included Rogers's client-centered therapy, Abraham Maslow's hierarchy of needs, Fritz Perl's gestalt therapy, and Rollo May's existential therapy, to name a few.

To Gendlin's surprise, he found that the particular style of therapy made little difference in predicting successful outcomes. Some clients did well and some not so well, no matter what the theoretical orientation and sometimes no matter what the skill of the therapist.

However, he found lasting positive change when clients could access a nonverbal, bodily feel for the problem that brought them to therapy in the first place. He called this intuitive feel a "felt sense." Over time, Gendlin began to suspect that the skill of identifying this felt sense could be taught.

In 1978 he published a little book called *Focusing* that described in nontechnical language how a layperson could connect with their felt senses and use them to guide personal growth. He described the way this skill could be learned — through six steps, or "movements":

1. *Clearing a space*
2. *The felt sense*
3. *Finding a handle*
4. *Resonating*

5. *Asking*
6. *Receiving*

The book quickly became a bestseller with over half a million copies in circulation. It was translated into seventeen different languages.

Deepening

In 1980 I joined a team of people who offered intensive four-day, cathartic weekend retreats. One member of the team was a psychologist who had trained with Gendlin. He taught some of us Focusing techniques.

At that time I already had a robust therapy practice. Another therapist colleague on the team and I recognized immediately how helpful Focusing could be for our clients. And we thought it had the potential to go further. Emotions are complex, with many layers, nooks, and crannies. There could be entangled strands that were not apparent at first glance. We realized it was valuable for clients not only to find a good label for their felt sense but to navigate it using their own preverbal feeling tones. This helped clients to create more space around their feeling tones, and sometimes even to dive right into their core.

So we began experimenting with techniques that could go more deeply into and through the felt senses and their hidden connections with other aspects of consciousness. We found that these practices deepened the therapy. Talking with each other, we fell into calling our evolving set of practices "Deepening."

Convergence of Therapy and Meditation

At that time I was about ten years into a Buddhist meditation practice. I had started teaching a few classes and mentoring individuals.

Meditators did not talk about feeling and relationship conflicts as much as therapy clients did. But their meditation did get bogged down in other things. There were "hindrances," or *nīvaraṇa*, that would disrupt their practice. Sometimes meditation followed a predictable track. Other times it went awry.

As I guided them, I instinctively brought in some of the Deepening practices. I was surprised that they seemed to work as well with meditators as they did with therapy clients.

As I look back on this convergence, perhaps I shouldn't have been surprised. Both therapy and meditation center on awareness and insight. Both have obstacles, which are called "neuroses" in therapy and "delusions" in meditation. When neuroses or delusions dissolve, the result is called "insight" in both arenas.

In therapy, the deepest problems are referred to as "character structures." In meditation, they are called "identity states." I suspected these terms were referring to the same thing, only using different terminology. Both fields had their own techniques, practices, and language, most of which sounded different on the surface but could be seen to be aligned underneath.

Despite these convergences, there were various strengths and weaknesses in each arena that did not overlap. For example, psychotherapy explored inner feelings in order to help the person feel better — this was like moving the furniture around in the room to make living easier. Meditation cared less about the furniture and more about getting out of the house entirely — seeing through the delusion of a separate self-essence in a universe that is deeply interdependent.

Psychotherapy tended to confuse deep equanimity with dissociation. Meditation tended to confuse dissociation with equanimity. Psychotherapy appreciated how strong the neuroses could be. Meditation underestimated how persistent delusions could be.

As I began to have more clients who were meditators and more meditation students who were clients, the Deepening process blended these two approaches so that the strengths in one made up for the weaknesses in the other. With this, my clients' and students' awareness and consciousness deepened more rapidly and smoothly.

Deepening has many practices, attitudes, and perspectives that I have described in other writings.[1] This booklet brings them together in an overarching framework that I have found helpful. As we go along, I will provide some references to techniques in Focusing and Buddhist meditation when they are clarifying. But my overall intent is to provide a practical, uncluttered guide to the Deepening process.

---

[1] See the Resources list on page 39.

1

Example Sessions

Nothing is difficult. Some things take time.
— David Darling

This chapter will explore a few examples of Deepening sessions. The next chapter describes various ways a session might unfold and how to facilitate it in ourselves or guide it for another person.

One of the difficulties in writing about Deepening or any interesting area of life is that feelings, ideas, and experiences interact in an interdependent web where everything directly or indirectly affects everything else. Meanwhile, a book marches through a linear sequence of ideas, stories, words, paragraphs, and chapters. This chapter emphasizes the broader picture. The next chapter examines specific details. If you prefer to learn the underlying principles of Deepening techniques before seeing the broader sweep of a session, you can skip ahead to the next chapter and come back to this one later.

Obviously, no two sessions are alike. They may vary in length from five or ten minutes to three-quarters of an hour or more. The following sessions are with someone I'll call "Billy." The first is the session in which I introduced Deepening to him.

The transcripts were reconstructed from notes I took at the time: they may not be exact. I purposely changed some nonessential details to protect his anonymity. But otherwise the dialogues unfolded roughly as presented. The ellipses ("...") indicate pauses of a few moments to several minutes.

Session One: Numbness to Hidden Calm

- Doug: For several months now we've been reflecting on your life, family, and meditation practice. I feel I've gotten to know you.

I wonder if we've come to the point where it might be helpful to experiment with another process that I call "Deepening." Rather than having you describe things you've already felt or experienced, we jump into the present and have you describe what's going on right now.

It may feel a little like meditation except for a sparse dialogue between us. I'll ask what's inside you. Your responses help me attune to your experience. Sometimes I'll make suggestions. But mostly you simply go inside and I tag along.

- *Billy: Sounds good. How does it work?*

- Doug: I'll invite you to settle into the moment and allow your awareness to turn gently inward. Once you have an inner felt sense of something, you can let me know. I'll guide you through cycles in which awareness goes from the "surface" of the experience to what is "inside," "behind," "within," or "underneath" it. As you notice the deeper phenomena, the cycle repeats: settling, noticing, going in deeper, and repeating. Does that make sense?

- *Billy: Yes.*

- Doug: Good.

- *B: How do I begin?*

- D: Close your eyes or let them come to rest someplace undistracted ... And notice what's inside.

This is not about controlling or evaluating experience. We simply want to see what comes up when we don't try to guide it in any particular way. It is purely noticing what arises without preference.

- B: *Got it.*
- D: Gently allow the body to settle into the here and now ...
Let your system settle.

...

What do you notice?

- B: *There is a lump in my throat.*
- D: Can you see the boundaries of the lump? ... how far it extends?
- B: *Yes. But as I observe it, it changes into a kind of numbness.*
- D: The fact of being aware allows feelings and sensations to shift. Change is part of being alive. As you begin to see something clearly, there are three things that can happen: (1) it stays the same; (2) it intensifies; or (3) something else comes up. We don't care which one of these occurs. We care more about following the mind-heart than directing or shaping it.

...

Is the numbness still there?

- B: *Yes ...*
- D: Let your awareness go into the center of the numbness

...

What do you see?

- B: *It feels more like sadness. There are tears. Sorrow ...*
- D: Let your awareness go into the sadness, tears, and sorrow .... Relax into the middle of them.
- B: *The sadness feels heavier ...*
- D: Just settle into the middle of the heaviness.

...

- B: *There are little hints of lightness. It's like a flickering that changes back and forth from heaviness and sadness to calmness*

...

Back and forth ...

- D: Is your awareness drawn to one more than the other?
- B: *It's drawn to the calm.*

• D: Let the awareness do as it wants. Gently open up to the calm without pushing the sadness away . . .

What do you notice?

• *B: The calm feels larger. It's like a circle of quiet with sadness around the edges.*

. . .

• D: Expand with it . . .

What's it like now?

B: It stays the same . . .

Now the calm is a little larger, then a little smaller, then larger again.

. . .

Now the calm seems like it's in front of the body.

• D: Just notice it floating out there, as it were.

• *B: There is a point of tension.* [He points to the place between his eyebrows.]

• D: Open to it all at once: the calm and the tension.

• *B: The calm keeps growing bigger.*

• D: Is the sadness still there?

• *B: Yes, but it has faded into the background . . . Barely perceptible . . .*

• D: Lovely. Just expand with the foreground . . .

We will run out of time in just a few minutes. But before I ask you to open your eyes, I would like to ask you a question . . .

Does the calm feel new or ancient or somewhere in between?

• *B: It feels like it's been there forever. I just forgot to notice it.*

• D: That's great.

Now that you feel it, just marinate in it for a few moments. Let it soak in . . .

Having a strong, embodied memory of how it feels will help you return here when you like.

. . .

And when you're ready, slowly open your eyes and see how that affects you.

. . .

Session Two: Dark Ocean to Clear Awareness

In the following weeks and months, Billy and I continued to speak together regularly about difficulties in his personal and family life and about his meditation practice. We did Deepening sessions during about half of those meetings. The following session took place about a year after the first and a few weeks after he'd undergone some minor surgery.

- D: Would you like to go in and look at these issues more directly?
- *B: Yes. That would probably be good.*
- D: Okay. You know the routine. Let your eyes rest. As you do so, see what's present just now. Our emphasis is on seeing clearly what's here rather than controlling awareness.
- *B: Right . . .*
- D: . . . What do you notice inside?
- *B: An endless, dark ocean.*
- D: Relax into it. Open up and see what's there.

. . . As you do this, let the awareness go into or underneath the dark ocean.

- *B: As deep as I can see, there is complete inertia . . . Shutdown . . . Despair.*
- D: It's okay. Keep surrendering into it.
- *B: Deep, dark sorrow . . . Wanting to hide and be small.*
- D: Go ahead: make yourself small . . .

What's it like to make yourself small? . . .

What would it be like to be smaller than you think possible? . . .

- *B: . . . [He says nothing, but his face relaxes a little.]*
- D: What happens?

- *B: I'm super small. Like I'm gone . . . Nothing there . . .*
- D: Be nothingness.
- *B: Now there's an ocean of calm darkness.*
- D: Be the ocean . . .

What does the ocean have to say to you?

- *B: . . .*

There are no words. Just a sense of quiet calm.

- D: Be with it. Expand into it . . .
- *B: . . .*

Now there's an emotional knot around Mickie [his son] *and Lynn* [his partner].

But there is calm in the middle . . .

- D: Just soften into the knot without pushing anything away.
- *B: . . .*

Expansion . . .

- D: Just notice . . .
- *B: Serenity spreads out.*

. . .

Now there's a touch of pain. [He touches the surgical site.]

- D: Let both the calm and the pain be as they are. They can coexist.
- *B: . . .*
- D: What happens?
- *B: Subtle.*

Completely quiet . . .

Absence of self . . .

- D: Be with all of that.
- *B: . . .*
- D: What is the awareness like right now?
- *B: Dark. Strong. Alert*

. . .

Sinking down.

Spreading out.

Expanding.

. . .

Completely quiet . . .

The body recedes.

- D: Savor

- B: *The sea of calm spreads out farther.*

. . .

The image of a bird in a field pops up and disappears.

. . .

Just nothing.

- D: Keep getting out of the way.

Let awareness be. If something shows up, let awareness take care of it on its own.

Let the mind rest in nothingness, emptiness, presence as much as it likes.

. . .

- B: *Now there's no darkness or heaviness — just clearness.*

- D: Expand and spread out.

- B: *. . .*

A little dullness creeps into the clearness.

- D: Observe without preference.

. . .

No need to fight it.

. . .

Merge with the fog. Become one with it.

- B: *Wide-open awareness of awareness.*

In the distance are all the parts of my life that we've been talking about. But here, there is just clear awareness.

- D: Where does the awareness come from?

- B: *It's all around.*

It doesn't come from anywhere.

• • •

• D: What's happening?

• B: *Nothing. Clear awareness. Nothing.*

• • •

• D: *[After a few minutes]* What do you notice now?

• • •

• B: *Nothing. Emptiness. Clear awareness.*

• • •

• D: *[After five minutes.]* What's arising?

• B: *Nothing at all. Just empty awareness.*

2

Going In

*Try to be mindful and let things take their natural
course. Then your mind will become quieter and quieter
in any surroundings. It will become still like a clear
forest pool. Then all kinds of wonderful and rare animals
will come to drink at the pool. You will see clearly the
nature of all things in the world.*

– Ajahn Chah

In this chapter we'll look at the individual elements that
come together to create the Deepening process. The core of
Deepening is the core of the Buddha's teachings: the Four
Ennobling Truths.[2] I summarize the first three as "turning
toward, relaxing into, and savoring or smiling."

The First Ennobling Truth is about understanding: to free
ourselves from suffering (*dukkha*), the Buddha said we must
understand it. We can't comprehend suffering if we are looking
away from it. It is wiser to turn our attention toward the
discomfort so we can see up close how it arises, hangs around,
and passes away.

When we do this, we recognize that suffering arises from
tension (*taṇhā*), which encourages us either to grasp things or
to push them away (*upādāna*). In the Second Ennobling Truth,
the Buddha said we must "abandon tension." The phrase

---

[2] They are often called "the Four Noble Truths." But in the original Pāli, the
word for "noble" is idiomatic. It refers to the one who uses the "truths"
wisely. So I prefer to call them the "Four Ennobling Truths."

sounds awkward in English. A more graceful way to say it is, "Relax." Yet "relax" can have an aversive connotation in English, so to make it clear, I like to say, "Relax into."

When uneasiness arises in meditation or daily living, it is wise to turn toward and relax into it so that the tension can be *released,* not ignored or shunned. I learned the same paradox in martial arts — during a fall, we protect the body by softening *with* the fall rather than stiffening *against* it. At first this may seem counterintuitive: we relax into our grief, irritation, confusion, pain, or other discomfort rather than trying to control them.

If this leaves us feeling better, the Buddha recommended we realize this (or "make it real") by savoring the good feeling and letting it soak into our being (the Third Ennobling Truth). If "turning toward" and "relaxing into" does not bring up wholesome feelings, we can use a Buddha half smile to trigger uplifted qualities.

I refer to these first three Ennobling Truths as "Three Essential Practices." A more robust version of these is a six-part movement called the Six Rs: Recognize, Release, Relax, Re-Smile, Return, Repeat. I have written extensively about the Three Practices and the Six Rs in meditation.[3] They are a way of responding wisely to hindrances and other disturbances that arise in meditation. They are also central to Deepening.

I rarely use the word "Deepening" in an actual session. Taken out of context, it may sound pretentious. Instead, I ask

---

[3] Doug Kraft, *Buddha's Map* (Easing Awake Books, 2013), pp. 145-57; *Befriending the Mind* (Easing Awake Books, 2019), pp. 17-19, 109-14; *Presence* (Easing Awake Books, 2023), pp. 61-69. You can also look in the Topical Index at www.easingawake.com/?p=TopicalIndex.

the person if they would like to "go in" as in "go more deeply into your experience."

If they would like to, the first thing I do is nothing. I may ask them to close their eyes, settle in, and be with whatever they experience without preferences. This roughly corresponds to Gendlin's first movement, "Clearing a space." However, I don't tell them to clear a space or quiet down. If they know how, they will. If they don't, I'd rather show them than try to tell them. Depending on the person, I may describe how to clear the space or use a metaphor or story to evoke how it feels:

- "If we try to quiet down using force of will, we get the trying, the force, and the will but not the quiet. It's like telling a rambunctious kid to sit down and shut up: the admonition is disquieting rather than soothing."
- "A Quaker elder said that meditation is like coaxing a basket of puppies to sleep. A puppy raises his head, so we softly stroke him until he quiets down. Then another sticks her head up. We gently pat her. Gradually the litter quiets down if we treat them with simple, quiet kindness."
- "The Buddha said that when we can see what is going on with enough clarity, we will know what to do and what not to do. Our intent is simply to see clearly without preferences."
- "The writer and speaker Byron Katie is fond of saying, 'If you fight reality, you lose, but only 100 percent of the time.' We want to see reality, not fight it."
- "Reality doesn't care about our likes and dislikes; it just is what it is. We are looking to see what is most real."

Going to the Center

After a few moments, I'll ask what they notice inside. This corresponds to the beginning of Gendlin's second movement about finding a felt sense. I ask if the feeling seems to reside mostly in one part of the body or is diffuse. If they say it seems to be in their shoulder, chest, belly, or some other specific place, I ask them to let awareness go into that area. Otherwise, they can let the feeling be more general as they relax into it.

I rarely ask them to go back and forth between the felt sense and their words as Gendlin does. If their language is not the best descriptor of their experience, it will clarify as the Deepening continues. Meanwhile, I'd rather have them focus on the feeling than on the precise word for it.

Regardless of what they describe, I encourage them to "turn toward" and "relax into" their inner experience. It is wisest to simply be with whatever arises and soften or surrender into it. Regardless of what they describe, I ask them to let awareness go right into the middle of that feeling. To support this, I may say a number of things:

- "If the feeling seems to be in one part of the body, explore its 'geography' — how far it extends around that area and how deeply it goes into the body."

- "How feelings appear from far away may be different from how they appear up close. How it feels on the surface may not be the same as how it feels deep inside. So let awareness go into the very center of the felt sense. This is the heart of the Deepening practice."

- "Awareness itself may cause the feeling to change. That is normal. One of three things can happen: (1) the felt sense stays the same; (2) it intensifies; (3) something else comes up. We are more interested in what the feeling does than in telling it what to do. So any of these three is fine. There is no way this process can go wrong. Simply notice what the experience is and how it shifts."

- "If you do not have a clear sense of the feeling/sensation, don't force it. Just be aware of the murkiness or fuzziness. It is just another feeling to be relaxed into."

- "If more than one feeling arises, you can see which one has the strongest draw and follow that. Otherwise it's fine to soften or expand into all of them at once."

Blockages

As we travel with our own experience or guide someone else, it is common to come to some blockage or barrier where the process seems to stop. The person may become confused, distracted, or feel they can't go on until they fix or change something. It can be frustrating and discouraging. To help loosen things up, I might suggest:

- "Turn toward and relax into the blockage itself. How does it feel? What's it like to be stuck? No matter what arises, let it be the focus of the Deepening process."

- "Shift your focus from the problem at hand to the awareness that is looking at the stuck-ness: how does that consciousness feel? Is it demanding, shy, enthusiastic, rough, expansive, pulled in? Is there tension in it? If so, 'turn toward' and soften."

- "If relaxing into it seems confining, try expanding or spreading out instead. 'Relaxing into,' softening, and expanding are all different ways of experiencing release and surrender. Use whatever works."

- "Often the label for an experience can be an umbrella term. What are the actual sensations beneath that umbrella term? What is the direct experience that leads you to give it that name?"

- "Emotions can feel like layers in which any feeling can mask another feeling. Affection may cover anger. Humor may mask discouragement. Shyness may hide enthusiasm. And so on. As Deepening continues, layers may peel away surprises underneath. That is normal. Enjoy the ride."

Recurring Experiences

It is not unusual for the progression of experiences to vary widely. Yet sometimes, the path circles back into a similar place. Circling back may be a sign that there is something subtler going on underneath.

I have a reverse-paranoia model of how the universe works: It's not trying to get us down. Rather the universe is trying to lift us up. If it keeps coming back to the same place, there is probably something subtler underneath that we are missing. It needs good attention. Awareness may keep bringing us back until we see it fully.

Unfortunately, the universe doesn't seem to care or even notice what we feel. If we are exhausted or tired or just don't want to deal with the issue anymore today, it doesn't get it. It just rubs our noses in it. So we have to bring wisdom to the process using the Three Practices.

Whatever we are missing may be subtle, or we would have spotted it before. So it helps to pay more attention to elusive flickers or faint impressions and then to turn awareness toward them and let go more fully into them.

When Practicing Rests

Ultimately, what the mind wants most is to know itself. Philosophical and theoretical speculation do little to satisfy this yearning. Awareness wants to know awareness up close and face-to-face. The process of getting to this can be complicated, but the actual knowing is simple. Lao Tsu wrote, "See simplicity in the complicated." Awareness won't rest until it has this simple knowing without intervening ideas.

Deepening at its best cuts through the complexity, quiets the running around, and is just aware of itself the same way we might be aware of a small child resting in our arms. Getting there may seem intricate, but being there is simple and ordinary:

   • For example, as you read these words there are probably
   several types of things going through your mind: the words you

are reading, the meaning they generate in your mind, other thoughts and images that reverberate from what you've experienced in the last day, week, or lifetime.

• Can you just open up to all of this? You don't have to do anything specific — just know the impressions are there, however sharp or vague. This is one of the meanings of "nondual awareness": having many things in the mind and memory at once without pushing or pulling any one of them.

• Can you relax into this quiet swirl?

• Back behind all these, can you feel a quiet place? . . . It does nothing to draw attention to itself. It is just there . . . It has always been there, though we may rarely see it because of distractions . . . Notice it now . . . Just lightly be with it.

• It has no content. It is awareness with nothing in it . . . Awareness of awareness.

• It is contented. Peaceful. It looks for nothing. It's happy in a simple, ordinary way.

• This is what the mind-heart wants most: to simply know itself.

The slightest thought or feeling or movement can obscure it like a fog obscuring the stars. But the stars are still there. The quiet doesn't go away just because our focus moved away. It remains patiently waiting for us to show up.

The Deepening practice at its best helps the heart quiet enough so we can notice this peace and well-being like stars appearing as the clouds drift away. Deepening does not create peace and well-being. It can't create them. They're always here.

The End of Practice

There are other practices that can help different people at different times. Forgiveness softens feelings of unworthiness that may be the residue of the doctrine of original sin that infected our culture centuries ago. Nondual awareness can broaden our view of life. Intuition, guidance, and surrender reveal wisdom we didn't know was available to us.

The Deepening techniques themselves often require only a few minutes before something starts to shift inside (though they can take longer). But these other practices often take more time. I've talked about forgiveness extensively elsewhere,[4] but not as much about the others.

The next chapter goes into the Spectrum of Awareness and how it relates to nondual awareness, intuition, guidance, and surrender. So if you are interested in those, stay tuned.

For now, let's look at the end of all these practices. When is it best to release them and just be? Sometimes when the mind-heart comes to a quiet place, we sense there is something more to explore, but now is not the time to go into it. It may be wiser to savor the touch of contentment and come back later.

Other times the mind-heart deepens into an easy stillness. If I am guiding someone in Deepening and ask, "What are you aware of now?" like Billy (pp. 15), they usually say, "Nothing. It's all still." Sometimes the quiet is palpable.

So I just sit silently with them, checking in with them occasionally to see where they are. Things might shift. As noted earlier, sometimes a peaceful layer uncovers a disturbance, which rises up and makes a fuss. Other times, the serenity stretches to the horizon and it's best just to savor it.

I have been impressed over the years that no matter where a person starts, if they keep relaxing into the core of their experiences, they come to a sense of well-being and

---

[4] Doug Kraft, *Buddha's Map* (Easing Awake Books, 2013), pp. 165-70, and on the web at www.easingawake.com/?p=ForgivingOurselves.

contentment. This seems to be the core of the core of each of us. This is where this practice comes to rest and the personal fades into the universal. It is a taste of enlightenment.

Pain and fear can also be strong and overwhelming. At times they seem impenetrable. But given enough openness to whatever arises, the deepest place seems to be this spacious contentment.

Whether it lasts for a few minutes, a few hours, or the rest of our life, it is the deepest place we can go. It is broad, quiet, and content.

And it's more accessible than most people imagine.

3

Spectrum of Awareness

> *The best way to control a cow*
> *is to put it in a larger meadow.*
> Shunryū Suzuki Roshi[5]

In this chapter we shift attention from the cow and sheep that frolic or grumble around inside us to the large meadow of awareness itself. Awareness has many elements, which range from the dense content of our thoughts to the nothingness out of which they arise. Table 1 offers a conceptual overview.

Table 1: Spectrum of Awareness

Element	Examples
1. Content	Thoughts, plans, stories, ideas, problems
2. Processes	Thinking, planning, arguing, daydreaming worrying, storytelling, figuring
3. Qualities of awareness	Clear, foggy, open, light, agitated, calm, fast, sluggish, sticky, spacious
4. Awareness of Awareness	Noticing awareness apart from its content, processes, or qualities
5. Nothingness	Emptiness, "winking out," *nirodha*, *nibbāna*

---

[5] Shunryū Suzuki, *Zen Mind, Beginner's Mind: Informal Talks on Zen Meditation and Practice* (Shambhala Publications) 1970.

Like most of Buddhism, the Spectrum of Awareness is a phenomenology. It's not a philosophy, theology, ontology, metaphysical paradigm, or intellectual construct. It's a *description* of direct experience (phenomena) rather than *ideas* about phenomena. The Buddha found that when we see clearly, that is enough to end suffering.

Content

The first element of the Spectrum of Awareness is content. The evolutionary function of awareness is to see the content of experience and develop a map of what's out there: bird, tree, rock, river, etc. Some objects have more charge: a guy with a spear, a dog with its teeth bared. The greater the charge, the more the mind shrink-wraps around the object and the more solid it feels. Looking at a quiet sunset on a beach, our mind lightens. Looking at a gale blowing off the ocean, our mind thickens.

Processes

As the mind-heart relaxes and expands, we may begin to notice the second element of the Spectrum: the processes out of which the content arises. We notice the thinking, feeling, daydreaming, and other mental actions rather than just the contents of thinking, feeling, daydreaming, etc.

The processes can be light (musing, wondering, fantasizing) or energized (complaining, worrying, arguing, exploring, defending). As the mind relaxes and expands, the contents drift into the background and the mental actions become clearer.

If I'm guiding someone who is caught up in a story or worry, I may suggest:

• "Let the awareness expand to include the processes in the mind. Don't push the content aside; let it be there. It may wander off into the foothills if it chooses. But you are not trying to make it do anything. Instead, you are expanding the field of awareness to include what the mind-heart is doing."

• "Here's a hint: Content usually focuses on the past or future — what happened a while ago or what might happen tomorrow. The processes only exist in the present. You may be worried about an upcoming job, but the worrying is happening now."

Qualities

Once we comfortably see the processes, it is relatively easy to notice the qualities of awareness that give rise to the processes. Awareness can be light, serene, peaceful, or easygoing. Or it may be more energetic: angry, fearful, urgent, excited, obsessive.

As we notice the qualities, the mind-heart naturally relaxes and expands. And it works the other way around as well: as the mind-heart relaxes and expands, we become more aware of the subtle qualities of awareness.

• As before, let the content and processes do what they want. If they wander off on their own, that's fine. But don't try to get rid of them; remain welcoming and let awareness rest in the qualities.

• The qualities are only found in the present. We may remember how they were a while ago or speculate about what will happen later. But we directly experience them now and only now.

Awareness of Awareness

As the qualities become more apparent, we may start to notice awareness itself, be it a large pasture or a small pen. We notice the effects of being aware. This is analogous to taking in an entire meadow rather than just zeroing in on the cows, plants, and terrain. On a smaller scale, it is like meeting a new person and being struck by their overall presence rather than just their freckles or socks; or taking in the ambience of a crowd rather than just a few individuals in the crowd.

Awareness of awareness is different from the previous elements in the Spectrum. Contents, processes, and qualities are "out there." As we move to qualities, we are observing subtler and subtler objects. But there is still a subject looking at objects. But with awareness of awareness, there are no external objects. Objectless awareness is looking at itself. It is pure subjectivity. And it feels very different.

We live in a culture and have inherited evolutionary tendencies that value objects. Many people come to believe that happiness comes from getting material stuff such as food, money, or gadgets; or immaterial stuff such as feelings, relationships, status, or lovely experiences. The formula says, "Happiness comes from getting things out there."

Objectless awareness feels different and is hard to put into words because language is about subjects and objects. Now we are moving into the nondual, where objects and objectivity are replaced by objectless awareness and pure subjectivity.

So rather than try to describe this objectively, it might be more helpful to evoke it experientially. Rupert Spira[6] is a teacher of nondual awareness. He offers contemplations that evoke nondual knowing. He suggests that we have two very different kinds of selves. One is the roles (or "persons") we adopt: parent, child, lover, activist, artist, worker, citizen, consumer, meditator, etc. These are dualistic. The other is the awareness that perceives all these persons and things. This is

---

[6] Rupert Spira is an English spiritual teacher, philosopher, proponent of the "Direct Path" of nondual awareness, and writer. He has extensive videos on www.YouTube.com.

nondual awareness of awareness. The following contemplation borrows from Rupert Spira and others. Ask yourself:

• Who am I really?

• There are lots of elements that can make up a sense of self. We'll go through them and set aside anything that is temporary or impermanent — anything that might change over time.

• It's as if you are taking off your clothes and setting aside anything that is transient. For example, your shoes; books; electronic devices; the contents of your cupboards, closets, and garage ... all the stuff in your life that will change or disappear sooner or later: your cars, your clothes, your home, your pets.... So set them aside.

• Now remove the immaterial stuff as well:

• Emotions come and go, thoughts arise and pass. So set them aside...

• Memories form and drift away...

• Relationships change inevitably: some childhood friends are long gone. Some new friends may not have arrived yet. Imagine all of them gone. ...

• There are many skills you have acquired, from walking to driving to playing the guitar to meditating. Imagine they're all gone. ...

• Aspirations, dreams, fears all come and go. Even your values and principles shift. Imagine them gone.

• If you could remove everything that is transient, would there be anything left? ...

• What's left is what has been observing all these things come and go throughout your life.

• Body sensations change. How you feel right now is not exactly the same as what you felt five minutes ago. Or five days ago. Or when you were five years old. But it feels as if what is watching all this is the same today as it was many years ago...

• We call this "me." It's the "I" that has observed all the stuff, feelings, memories, relationships, and so on that have been coming, etc. ...

• This observer feels unchanged.

• Don't worry about the philosophical arguments about the existence or nonexistence of self — *anattā*. Just see if there is a phenomenon of a sense of self that is here and now observing the transience of your life. It was here a few minutes ago. And a few years ago ...

• The unchanging sense of "me" or "I" that observes is simple awareness ...

• If we strip out of awareness all its content, processes, and qualities, we are left with awareness itself: we are aware of awareness.

• What is this simple awareness like? ...

• What are the qualities of this unchanging me-ness? ...

When I do this contemplation or ask others to try it, and then ask what that awareness is like, typically it feels unruffled, steady, peaceful, happy, content. It's everything we really wanted in life and it's right here. It's been here all the time.

This is similar to the exercise I suggested in chapter 2 (p. 23) of looking behind all the thoughts, plans, images, and chatter in the mind and noticing if there is a place that is simple and peaceful. This, too, is awareness of awareness. It's a quiet observer.

These are the roots of enlightenment. And they are not out there. They have been with us all our life.

• See if you can touch into that place, even if just a few moments at a time. Let it seep into your being. Savor.

This is awareness of awareness.

Nothingness

Is there anything beyond awareness of awareness?

Staring into the sky on a dark night, it is easy to see the stars. But we usually overlook the void that surrounds them.

However, without the emptiness of outer space, there would be nothing to contain the stars and planets. Nothing could exist.

Similarly, it is easy to see the content, processes, and qualities but to overlook the emptiness that makes them possible. But we don't have to. When looking into a moonless night, we can see the empty space between the stars rather than just the celestial objects.

> • If your mind is quiet and still for a while and then starts to chatter, you can turn your awareness to the chatter. Or you can look back into the emptiness out of which the chatter arose and let attention rest on this stillness.

Winking Out

If we are aware of awareness and continue to relax and expand, we may notice the nothingness out of which phenomena and awareness arise. In meditation, these sometimes manifest as a short, blank spot in our attention. I affectionately refer to this as "winking out" because it feels similar to nodding off without knowing it.

However, when we nod off and come back, the mind is often a little dense, foggy, or drifty. But as the mind-heart relaxes and expands, there may be blank spots followed by awareness that is light, clear, and still. It's unlikely that we actually fell asleep. There is another, more likely explanation.

It takes a little effort to turn raw sensation into an identified perception. And it takes a little effort to push an experience into the memory banks. When the mind-heart gets deeply relaxed, perception and memory stop operating. Even the perception of the passage of time is gone. We can't tell if we winked out for a moment or for an hour.

The Buddha referred to some kinds of winking out as "nirodha": the cessation of perception, feeling, and consciousness. When winking out is deep enough, the mind-heart that returns is not exactly like the one we once knew. The objects, concepts, and sense of self that once predominated have receded far into the background of irrelevance. This is a sign of nibbāna — a topic for another time.

Intuition

From the perspective of the awareness, we have relaxed and expanded from one end of the Spectrum to the other. At the high end of the Spectrum the Buddhist texts say that we become "independent in the Dhammā," meaning that we can know what is most helpful without teachers. Our own intuition can guide us even when other people can't. When we take care of the Dhammā, the Dhammā takes care of us. The perspectives of friends and teachers can still be valuable. But we have access to wisdom on our own.

Intuition can be cultivated and refined. There are many ways to do this. Here is a simple one:

- Think of a question you yearn to know more about. The longing draws the intuition, so let it be a genuine query for which you don't know the answer. The best questions are nuanced rather than black or white, yes or no. They can be simple: "What's next?" "What can help me go deeper?" "What's the best way to view this issue?" Relax into your question.

- Then imagine standing on the edge of what you know and speaking your questions from the heart into the unknown, emptiness, or nothingness.

- Rest there for a few minutes.

- Then release the question. Let it drop away and go back to your meditation or daily life.

- Let the answers come to you in their own time and way. Sometimes a response comes quickly. Other times it takes a while and may catch you when you aren't expecting it. Patience helps.

In speaking about contemplative prayer, a Christian saint observed, "Many people have enough faith to pray to God, but few have enough to listen."

Whether we imagine this process as one of talking to God, or to the still small voice, or to the universe, emptiness, or nothingness ... afterward it feels like listening with the heart. It helps to keep yourself out of the way and just listen humbly to the unknown. Receive.

If the language I have used does not resonate with you, sense what it points to, find your own language, and let it flow. Receive.

Of course, when we open ourselves up in this way, it is possible for old, suppressed delusions and neuroses to waltz in disguised as monks and wizards. So before we divorce our partner, quit our job, or give all our savings to charity, it helps to sit with the guidance and run it through the rational mind. If what we heard was wisdom, it will survive the scrutiny. Or we can use our doubts or misgivings to frame another question: "Did I get that right?" "Is there a nuance I am missing?" Etc.

As we cultivate and exercise our intuition, we'll begin to see when it comes through clean and when it may be distorted a little or a lot. We get better with practice.

At the high end of the Spectrum of Awareness and the high end of the *jhānas*, things get simpler and more ordinary. And the most important aspects of Deepening and meditation are relaxing, cultivating intuition, and getting out of the way.

All three of these involve surrender: the topic of the next chapter.

4

Surrendering into Joy

We must walk consciously only part way toward our goal, and then leap in the dark to our success.
— Henry David Thoreau

There are 100 billion stars in our galaxy and two trillion galaxies in the universe. Scientists' best guess is that one star in five has an earth-like planet. Even if there is only one in a thousand, that is an astronomical number of earth-like environments.

It is reasonable to assume there is a lot of intelligent life out there and it is silly to assume that humans are the most evolved creatures in the universe. There must be Yoda-like species who are not only smarter and more technologically advanced than we are but whose consciousness is more subtle and complex than we can know. The consciousness of such beings may be as hard for us to grasp as it is for turkeys to grasp human consciousness. For more evolved beings, what we see as the apex of spiritual practice may be just a starting point. What we see as advanced may be rudimentary for them.

The highest forms of consciousness are ones we feel more than ones we can figure out or think our way into. The height of Buddhist practice has to do with direct experience more than with understanding, with intuition more than with cognition, and with surrender more than with mere relaxation.

Brahmavihāras

There are a lot of Buddhist practices that point toward surrendering into joy.

Intellectually, the central teaching of Buddhism is Dependent Origination. This sees us and everything around us embedded in an interdependent web of relationships — like a gigantic, three-dimensional spiderweb in which everything either directly or indirectly affects everything else. Science teaches this as well. But the fruits of Buddhist practice are not merely scientific, intellectual, or conceptual understandings. They require the direct knowing and experiencing of these understandings deep inside.

One way to experience this depth relies on the *brahmavihāras*. "Brahmavihāra" is a Pāli word meaning "sublime abode" or "uplifting consciousness." In these states we feel very little tension or feel the releasing of tension.

While there are actually many brahmavihāras, traditionally there are four: *mettā, mudita, karuna,* and *upekkhā*. Let's look at them.

The root of the term "mettā" is *"maitrī"* which means "friend." It points to the feeling of friendliness or kinship.

"Mudita" is a Pāli term often translated as "sympathetic joy." It evokes the uplift one feels when seeing someone enjoying life. It's what we feel while watching a young child giggling as she chases soap bubbles across the lawn or when we empathize with a cat purring serenely in our lap. Mudita is the spontaneous joy that arises upon encountering the well-being of another.

"Karuna" is usually translated as "compassion" and is described as "the outflowing of the heart in response to another's suffering." Again, it's something we feel more than think about. It is a heart-centered quality like mettā and muditā but can be more difficult to work with because it resonates with suffering rather than friendliness or well-being. We may feel sad.

Strong sadness can turn into poignancy. Feeling alone can soften into feeling others as part of ourselves. The videographer and author John Koenig describes this shift:

> *The word sadness originally meant "fullness," to be filled to the brim with some intensity of experience. It's not about despair, or distraction, or controlling how you're supposed to feel, it's about awareness. Setting the focus to infinity and taking it all in, joy and grief all at once; feeling the world as it is, the world as it could be. The unknown and the unknowable, closeness and distance and trust, and the passage of time. And all the others around you who are each going through the same thing.*[7]

With this, our sense of separateness fades a little. We may not call it "surrendering into joy," but there is a tenderness of spirit that can be enriching and expansive.

The last of the four classical brahmavihāras is upekkhā which is usually translated as "equanimity."

Notice that the first three brahmavihāras are slightly different responses to people depending on their condition: friendliness with someone who we feel is on a par with us; joy with someone who is feeling wonderful; and compassion with someone who is suffering.

As the sadness of compassion expands into poignancy, we may find we feel an inner balance no matter what the other

---

[7] John Koenig, *The Dictionary of Obscure Sorrows*, (Simon and Schuster, 2021), eBook Edition. This passage was taken from the website: www.thedictionaryofobscuresorrows.com.

person's condition. The German philosopher Martin Heidegger
put it this way:

> *Imagine an awareness that sees to the heart of suffering*
> *with no urge to fix anything. Imagine this awareness is the*
> *opposite of indifference.*

The opposite of indifference is love. In this case, it's a
loving equanimity or sense of oneness.

Taken together, the brahmavihāras suggest how the
Buddha might have felt. Stated formally, his teaching began
with the First Ennobling Truth of suffering. He said the
suffering we feel is baked into existence. It's not our fault. He
was looking for a way to feel unburdened by it.

His solution was simple: if the suffering can't be fixed,
maybe we can get rid of the sufferer? If there is no one to
suffer, then there is no suffering. Only the Buddha went one
step further. Rather than get rid of the self, he suggested
looking deeply into the phenomena of self until we see that
there is no self-essence.

One famous simile describes breaking a chariot down into
its component parts: pole, axle, wheels, ropes, seat, etc. [8] We
can't find the chariot itself in any of those parts. Yet when the
components are put together, we have a chariot. We can ride
around in it, but it has no essence. It is said to be empty of
chariot-essence.

Similarly, the self is a construction of many different parts.
But we can't find the self in our toe, or elbow, or nose. We can't
find it in our thoughts or feelings or any other phenomena
associated with ourselves. Therefore, the self is just a
convention that refers to a collection of parts.

---

[8] The simile is found in the Buddhist text "Milindapañha" *or* "Milinda's
Questions" which is part of the *Khuddaka Nikāya* of the *Tipitaka*.

If you want to explore this further, try this:

• Take anything that you think of as part of you and trace it back to its origins.

• Where did it come from?

• Whether it is something physical like your thumb or something immaterial such as your fondness for certain foods or people, trace backward to see where that came from.

• Then trace back farther to see where those sources came from.

• And the sources' sources.

The interdependent web of life is constantly morphing and changing. We are only a momentary configuration that has no real stability or essence apart from everything in the web.

Yes, the idea of an independently existing chariot and the self are useful conventions. But both are empty of any essence that sets them apart from everything else.

When we see this, there is joy. It's not our joy. It's the joy that is uncovered when we realize there is no self that needs protection.

> *We live in illusion and the appearance of things. There is a reality. We are that reality. When you understand this, you see that you are nothing. And, being nothing, you are everything. That is all.*
>
> – Kalu Rinpoche

Beyond Knowing

The brahmavihāras are not the only way to evoke surrendering into joy. For example, in the previous chapter, the subtlest element of the Spectrum of Awareness is nothingness or no-thing-ness: there are no separate things, just a flow of living.

The jhānas are another example of a path to surrender. The high end of the jhāna experience is pretty simple. It is a deeper and deeper releasing. The relaxation is so complete that we even let go of the urge to understand or know what is going on. We soften, expand, and surrender.

One of the hallmarks of the eighth jhāna is wondering whether we're awake or dreaming. It's hard to discern. Images may flicker through the mind without weaving into a coherent narrative. If we tighten up just a little, the dreamy quality and the flickering images are gone. But if we surrender deeply, they may come back on their own.

(Note: this is not the same as the fog of sloth and torpor. It is quite the opposite. The awareness itself feels clear even when there is no content in it.)

Beyond the jhānas is nirodha: we wink out completely. There are no concepts, words, or perceptions left. As noted in chapter 2 (pp. 33), there are blank spots in which content disappears, including awareness of awareness. There is nothing, not even the sense of the passage of time.

Beyond nirodha is nibbāna: we enter nibbāna without knowing it. We only get hints of it when we return to normal consciousness and find everything feels different. What happened? We don't know. It's beyond us even to remember. Yet now life seems different and so much simpler.

To move into the highest and deepest awareness available to us, we have not just to relax and expand but to surrender our sense of self and even the urge to be aware. The highest human awareness is no awareness — a paradoxical unconscious awareness, if you will.

The shift from normal, everyday cognition to nibbāna is not conceptual. Feeling tone leads the way. Hypothetical beings out there who are more evolved than us would not just be ever more rapid thinking machine; rather they would use advance emergent instinctual intuition that we can no more understand than a badger can understand Shakespeare or a gerbil can grok Mozart.

Albert Einstein once said, "I did not arrive at my understanding of some of the fundamental laws of the universe through the power of the rational mind." His genius was twofold. First, he was able to directly intuit some of those fundamentals. Second, he was able to translate them into mathematical equations.

Meanwhile, in meditation, one difficulty with deep relaxation is quietly thinking we know or at least kind of know what this releasing is like. But we have to surrender even that gentle aspiration in order to wink out (see pp. 33). We have to surrender awareness.

Even if we get it that we can't really get it, it is still beyond us. We surrender our sense of self and the sense of knowing what we're doing. And when we come back, life feels quietly joyful. We have surrendered into joy.

A friend of mine described her first experience on a high-ropes course. While hanging by ropes, she was told to release her hold on one platform so she could swing over to the next. She said that being 99 percent committed to letting go was sheer terror. Being 100 percent committed was sheer joy.

Sidebar: Serendipity

It's not that we surrender for the sake of getting joy. It's not that joy is "out there" and surrendering brings us closer to it.

That would be complicated and involve desire (subtle craving) for joy. Rather, we surrender because holding on or holding back hurts subtly (or not so subtly). We surrender for the sake of surrender.

As our nervous system quiets down, it becomes more receptive to the ease and well-being that has quietly been there all along. As we let go, there is at least a tiny pause before the joy becomes known. It may come slowly.

If we surrender with "strings attached" — that is surrender with the expectation of joy — it may not work. Rather, we surrender because nothing else makes sense. Surrender is not a means to an end. It is an end in and of itself. If joy arises, that's serendipity.

Surrender Surrender

In the quote at the beginning of the chapter, Henry David Thoreau said, "We must walk consciously only part way toward our goal, and then leap in the dark to our success." Sometimes we leap. And sometimes we just let go into surrender.

To guide someone in this direction I might say:

• Close your eyes for a few moments ...
Let everything settle ...

• Let everything go. Relax. Soften. Expand. Surrender even knowing what you are doing ...

• Go for it, even if it seems a little crazy. Let go. Dissipate. Surrender.

• Surrender the images in your mind.

• Surrender commentary and storytelling.

• Surrender self, worry, fear, doubt, preferences.

• Surrender knowing.

- Surrender being right.
- Surrender attainment.
- Surrender awareness.
- Surrender being.
- Surrender surrender.

5

Maturing

See simplicity in the complicated.
— Lao Tsu

Deepening evolves. The most dramatic changes are the by-products of maturation. Changes are inevitable and can be likened to the natural fact that the flora, fauna, and topology of the lower regions don't resemble what we find at higher elevations.

In the beginning, we may imagine that spiritual practice is going to take us upward in a straight line, like a superhighway cutting through the hills. However, once we're higher up, we find that the path is more like a mountain trail that turns one way and then another as it follows the contours of the landscape. We eventually realize that it is simpler, faster, and more satisfying to enjoy the terrain as we progress than to exhaust ourselves building bridges and digging tunnels. At the peak there may be no discernible path at all. In the beginning we have goals. Toward the end, goals fade into irrelevance.

Deepening is a spiritual path that changes as it climbs. We already saw this in the Spectrum of Awareness (chapter 3), where the focus of awareness shifted from the content of awareness, to the processes that create that content, to the qualities that give birth to the processes, to pure awareness itself that carries all those qualities, and to the emptiness out of which awareness arises. We also saw in Surrendering into Joy (chapter 4) how the sense of self lightened and joy became more obvious.

In this chapter we'll note three other aspects of Deepening that morph as it matures. As shown in Table 2, these aspects are structure, views of hindrances, and our attitudes toward experience and the path itself.

Table 2: Some Ways Deepening Evolves

Spectrum of Awareness:	Content ▸ Process ▸ Qualities ▸ Awareness Itself ▸ Emptiness
Structure:	Complex ▸ Simple ▸ Empty
View of Hindrances:	Pests ▸ Visitors ▸ Getting Ourselves Out of the Way
Attitude toward Experience:	Curiosity & Inquiry ▸ Receptivity ▸ Nonself

Structure

The brain is a construction machine that builds models of the world (and ourselves) to help us better navigate our lives. The models can be quite complex and multilayered: the brain models simple objects (such as body parts), which come together with other objects to form complex objects (such as people), which come together to form families of objects (such as societies), which over time evolve cultures and whole ecosystems. Similarly, spiritual practices may seem complex as the brain constructs layers of perceptions, beliefs, practices, and worldviews.

The Deepening practice may likewise seem multifaceted, with many things flowing through the mind-heart all at once along with all the hidden layers that make up those things. As we "travel up the mountain," some things come to seem less important and fade away. The practice gets simpler and feels more ordinary. In the most advanced practice, everything fades.

This means that, in general, the Deepening practice evolves from complexity to simplicity to emptiness. But that emptiness allows subtle movements to surface and make the mind-heart seem more complex for a time. So while the overall trajectory is toward nothingness, the week-to-week and moment-to-moment flow has its ups and downs. We are wise to recognize these and adapt to what's present in any given moment.

Hindrances

This side of enlightenment, uninvited guests show up inside. We sometimes all them "hindrances" and often view them as "pests" to be gotten rid of. When they are complex, the Six Rs are an effective way of dealing with these itinerant visitors.

But as Deepening progresses, the complexities of the Six Rs can feel clunky and sluggish. The Three Practices feel simpler, more efficient, and more natural — turning toward, relaxing into, and savoring or smiling. We come to see that hindrances show us areas that need wholesome attention, not scorn.

Higher in the practice, even the Three Practices give way to just softening the distraction by softening the tension within them. At the highest altitudes in meditation or Deepening, it is best to get out of the way and let awareness take care of the errant visitors.

Attitude

These same considerations apply to the attitude with which we view our experiences and the path itself. At first, we greet experience with curiosity and active inquiry. This helps us engage the mind-heart wisely. But as we Deepen, peace emerges, rendering curiosity and inquiry a little too coarse because they encourage awareness to look at some experiences and overlook others. Some of our deepest insights arise from unexpected places. So, effective Deepening shifts from inquiry to simple receptivity without any agenda. We let the practice bring experience to us rather than going after anything specific.

Toward the mountaintop, we see that our receptivity is subtly influenced by whom we imagine ourselves to be — our sense of self decides what to look for and where to look. So we let the sense of self fade. In other words, our attitude goes from active engagement to passive receptivity to nonself. As with other aspects, attitude may fluctuate from day to day and moment to moment. If we see this fluctuation, we can adjust wisely.

Last Words

It's not surprising that Deepening changes as it matures. Life is fluid and ever-changing in subtle and not-so-subtle ways. It's less like a stone and more like a breeze, the tides, or the breath. When all movement stops, we are pronounced dead. But when we are alive, life and Deepening ebb and flow.

When I started writing this booklet, I intended to pin down exactly what Deepening is. As I come to these last pages, I confess I have failed.

Eugene Gendlin never pinned down exactly what he meant by "felt sense." He left it a little vague to give people room to sense it for themselves. When I was first studying Focusing, this ambiguity annoyed me. Today I have more sympathy for Gendlin.

The best I can do is to say that Deepening is a preverbal turning-toward, relaxing, softening, expanding, savoring, dropping, loving, half-smiling, ordinary, simple, nondual, inspiring, settling, intimate, universal, gradually unfolding moment.

Did you get that?

If not, the best I can do is to turn the last words over to the contemplatives and poets:

> *Wisdom says I am nothing.*
> *Love says I am everything.*
> *Between the two my life flows.*
>
> — Sri Nisargadatta

> *A foolish consistency is the hobgoblin of little minds,*
> *adored by little statesmen and philosophers and divines.*
> *With consistency a great soul has simply nothing to do.*
>
> — Ralph Waldo Emerson

> *The human soul is always moving outward into the*
> *objective world or inward into itself; and this movement*
> *is double because the human soul would not be conscious*
> *were it not suspended between contraries. The greater*
> *the contrast the more intense the consciousness.*
>
> — William Butler Yeats

> *To know me*
> *Is to breathe with me*
> *To breathe with me*
> *Is to listen deeply*
> *To listen deeply*
> *Is to connect*
>
> — Miriam Rose Ungunmerr Baumann

> *All goes onward and outward,*
> *Nothing collapses*
> *And to die is different from*
> *What anyone supposes*
> *And luckier.*
>
> — Walt Whitman

Resources

Bhante Vimalaraṁsi, *Moving Dhamma, Volume 1*. (Dhamma Sukha Meditation Center, 2012).

Doug Kraft, *Buddha's Map: His Original Teachings on Awakening, Ease, and Insight in the Heart of Meditation* (Blue Dolphin Publishing, 2013).

———, *Befriending the Mind: Easing into the Heart of Awakening* (Easing Awake Books, 2019).

———, *Circling Home: Spirituality Through a Unitarian Universalist Lens* (CreateSpace, 2010).

———, *Presence: Quiet Awareness and How It Emerges in Meditation and the Brain* (Easing Awake Books, 2023).

———, *Resting in the Waves: Welcoming the Mind's Fluidity* (Easing Awake Books, 2020).

Easing Awake website: http://www.easingawake.com.

Sayadaw U Tejaniya, *Awareness Alone Is Not Enough*, (Auspicious Affinity, 2008), http://www.ashintejaniya.org.

www.ingramcontent.com/pod-product-compliance
Lightning Source LLC
Chambersburg PA
CBHW070458050426
42449CB00012B/3030